Test Your Cat's Psychic Powers

Other Books by Missy Dizick

Test Your Cat's Mental Health
Cats Are Better Than Dogs

Test Your Cat's Psychic Powers

by
Missy Dizick

Adams Media Corporation
Holbrook, Massachusetts

Published by Adams Media Corporation
260 Center Street, Holbrook, MA 02343

ISBN: 1-58062-067-1

Printed in Hong Kong

J I H G F E D C B A

Library of Congress Cataloging-in-Publication Data
Test your cat's psychic powers / by Missy Dizick.
p.   cm.
ISBN 1-58062-067-1
1. Cats—Humor. I. Title.
PN6231.C23D594   1998
741.5'973—dc21   98-7884
                                CIP

This book is available at quantity discounts for bulk purchases.
For information, call 1-800-872-5627 (in Massachusetts, 781-767-8100).

Visit our home page at http://www.adamsmedia.com

This book is dedicated to my dear husband Ron, who has never once complained about Loulou sleeping under the covers. I also want to thank him for his support during the obsessive part of finishing the illustrations, which even extended to cooking dinner. Also, our loyal readers should know that he is the person responsible for the hilarious SPOOK scale, written as his official self, psychologist Ronald E. McKinney Ph.D.

Many thanks to our friend Karen Alexander Ph.D., a specialist in the paranormal, who advised, lent books, and brainstormed with us in the writing of this highly technical diagnostic tool.

And many thanks to Elvis for the idea.

INTRODUCTION

Does your cat spend quite a bit of time staring into space, just as though there is something out there? Does he always disappear on Halloween? If the coffee is disgusting, may kitty have given the coffee pot the evil eye? If so, it is most likely that your cat has psychic powers!

Try giving your beloved cat the following test. Note that for some items, it may be necessary to consult a friendly neighborhood psychic (unless you are one yourself), or to find one of the many aliens among us to assist in making the evaluation. Also, some items, such as hauntings, are reserved for those who are evaluating dear friends who have already passed beyond.

Add up your cat's score, and then consult the SPOO/K (Space, Psychic, Odd Occurrences/Kitties) Scale at the end of the book to see if your cat is a sensitive, a probable alien, or (most common) simply possessed by demons.

AURAS

Green (happy)

Rainbow (confused)

Red (angry)

Orange (sexy)

Blue (third eye power)

Yellow (open)

Black (evil)

Purple (spiritual)

BEING ABDUCTED BY ALIENS

Seen in vision, trance, hypnosis, dreams, or flashbacks . . . **10 pt.**
Direct observation. . . **50 pt.**

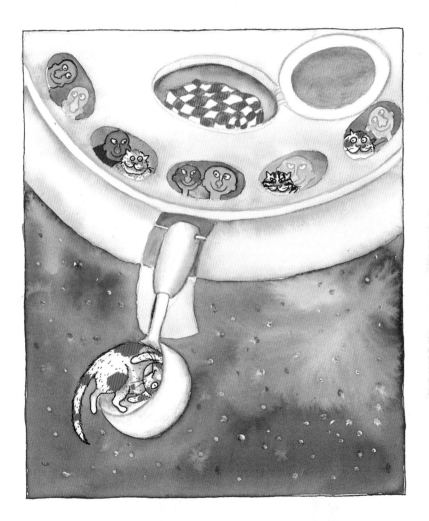

CAUSING ILL LUCK

Crab grass

Stains on the carpet

Checkbook imbalance

Flat tire

Bad dreams

CLAIRVOYANCE

Knows cat food
en route home

Knows crony has rat

Knows when someone is eating ice cream, even if asleep on roof

Knows dog out in rain

DEMATERIALIZE AND REMATERIALIZE

Under couch

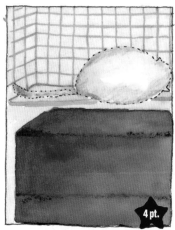

Top shelf

Under TV

Behind microwave

Rematerialize

DEMONIC POSSESSION

Roll around on floor with
hair standing up

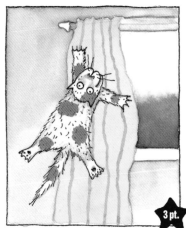

Fly up drapes

Race madly around house chasing nothing
(bonus 20 pts if on your bed at 4 A.M.)

Bring in snake

Eat the snake

Needs exorcism

GIVE THE EVIL EYE

To inferior cats

To the dog

To meter reader

2 pt.

4 pt.

5 pt.

To visitors

To the vet

To the coffee pot, causing coffee
to be nasty (specialty of black cats)

GUARDIAN SPIRITS

Kitchen

5 pt.

Computer

7 pt.

House

HAVING AN ALIEN'S LITTER OF KITTENS

Kittens with twisty tails

Six or more toes

Green hyperactive kittens

Conehead kittens

HEALING POWERS

Chilblains

Back pain

Flu

Hiccups

Tension headaches

HAUNTINGS

Couch   1 pt.

Garbage can   2 pt.

Dryer   3 pt.

Dog   5 pt.

Cat food

Child's sandbox

Humble

Unenlightened

A higher plane may exist

Will seek the higher plane

Truth seeker

All is revealed—there is no higher self than moi

IMMUNITY TO PAIN

2 pt.

Walking on coals

4 pt.

Unrequited love, as long
as the food keeps coming

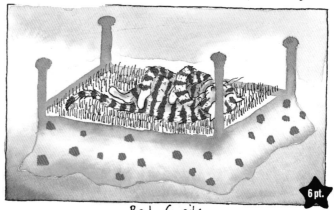

6 pt.

Bed of nails

Word problems in math

REAL loud music

WHY CATS JOIN ALIENS

Better chow

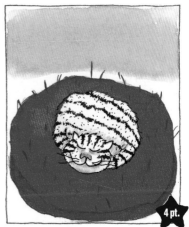

Better bed

Better kitty litter

Better kitchie-koo

To be with others of their kind

LAYING ON OF PAWS

2 pt.

Lays paws on stitches across eye

4 pt.

Abscess on other cat

6 pt.

Leg cast

Body cast

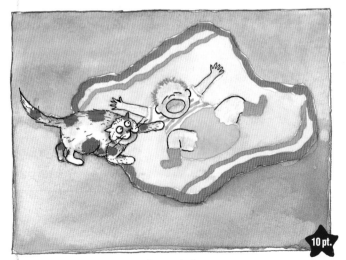

Colicky baby

LEVITATION

Top shelf of linen closet

Over table

Over top of fridge

Chandelier

Tree top

MEOWING IN TONGUES

50 bonus points

MIND-READING

Knows when being put out

Knows who's good for a handout

Knows who doesn't like cats

Knows who's allergic

Automatic writing—"Time to feed the pussycat"

Ouija board—"F-E-E-D-T-H-E-C-A-T"

Table thumping—"feed the kitty now"

Seance—"How many times I got to tell you—
FEED THE CAT!"

MESSAGES FROM OUTER SPACE

Take me to your leader

2 pt.

Disregard strange phenomena

5 pt.

Go to bed—time for an alien visitation

8 pt.

Go to clearing for teleportation

NEAR DEATH EXPERIENCES (NINE PER CAT)

Fight with big cat

Fight with big dog

Fall out window

Swimming pool

Playing chicken with car

OUT-OF-BODY EXPERIENCES

Indoor: Observes self in usual activities

Sleeping on bed

Sleeping on table

Outdoor out-of-body experience (more powerful)

POLTERGEISTS
Mischievous spirits, often attracted to cats and adolescents

Kibble flies across the room

Water dish jumps into air

Dishes fall out of cupboard and break

Runs in all pantyhose

PRECOGNITION

foresees trip to vet

foresees clean
laundry for nap

foresees wet paint to walk in

Nest of mice in pantry

Foresees bird flying smack into window

RECEIVING ORDERS FROM ALIENS

Antennae up for reception

Spill perfume

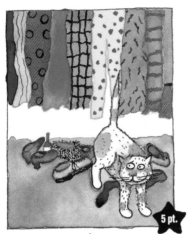

Hide
Tabasco sauce

Hide fuzzy slipper
(won't find until summer)

Hide car keys permanently

RECOLLECTION OF PAST LIVES

Was Martha Washington's cat

Was Good Queen Bess's cat

Was cat of Whistler's mother

Early Egyptian—pharaoh's cat

LATE Egyptians really got it right—
worshipped me as a goddess

RETURN OF ALIEN MESSAGES

Raise hair

Drink Cokes through straw

Eat chips and salsa

10 pt.

Lie flat on back with all four feet in air

SEEING VISIONS

Other cats who are not there

Invisible dogs

About a zillion rats

Unicorns in garden

TALK TO AN ANGEL

Learn a dog secret

Receive good advice

Update an angel

Update Grandma

Solve an old mystery

Find out where bodies are buried
(mice, rats, gophers, birds)

TELEKINESIS

Removes own collar

Ties shoelaces together

Ties knot in dog collar

Opens can of cat food

Opens all the cans of cat food

TELEPATHY

You should eat broccoli
and cabbage

Give your hot dog
to the cat

Share your ice cream
with the cat

Gopher! Come out
so I can devour you

Everyone feed me (more powerful)

TELEPORTATION

Causes butter dish
cover to rise

Uncovers cookies

Causes other cats to twirl
and flop

Gets best sweater out of
drawer for nap time

Large rock flies onto opponent's tail

Hamburgers fly into cat dish

TRANCES
(DIFFICULT TO TELL FROM NAP TIME)

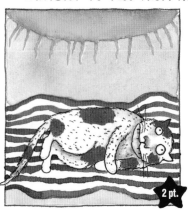

Put in trance by sunlight

By frog

Evil spirits

By bird feeder

By TV, along with human couch potato

WITCHCRAFT

Is a familiar

Casting spells, such as turning dog into mouse

Flying through air

Causes milk to curdle

5 pt.

Causes soufflés to fall—
also biscuits and cake

7 pt.

Rides shotgun on Halloween

15 pt.

Spacey—Psychic—Odd Occurrences—
Kitties—Scale

SPOO/KS
A Rating of Psychic Power

Scores
High (320—400)

Yours is a heavy responsibility indeed! You have been
entrusted with the care and feeding of a truly psychic
pussycat! You undoubtedly need no outside verification
that special, unusual, and even weird things go on in
and around your house on a regular basis. The challenge
is for you to determine if your pet wants you to be
privy to its special mission on this planet. Should you
betray your awareness when such is not permitted,
the consequences could be disastrous. Conversely, when
you and your pet share this heavy responsibility, great
achievements can ensue. Caution is the watchword. Also,
try to use this heavy responsibility by insuring that
your cat uses its powers mostly for good. Getting even
with your neighbors may be fun and satisfying, but our
experience is that powers misused in this way can turn

around and bite you back. True psychics, aware of their power, are usually benevolent—they can afford to be.

Moderately High (239—319)

Your cat may be on its progression toward being a true "sensitive." Also, it may have lost some of its previous power, either through disuse, misuse, or even from the evil acts of jealous competitors. You may be unprepared or unwilling to be responsible for a highly sensitive, psychically powerful kitty, and therefore you may choose to do nothing to aid in this journey. We counsel against this. Friends of ours did this and their fortunes and happiness suffered grievously from backlash of a still quite powerful and now angry possessor of special arts. Their only son was turned into . . . a lawyer! Meanwhile, be comfortable in the awareness that your special tabby is busily performing the mission on this planet with which it was entrusted. Should your cat's powers be on the wane from a previously higher level, be specially gentle to your unfortunate feline friend, who is likely to be quite embarrassed. You know how proud our cats can be.

Medium (Average) (158—238)

The fact remains inescapable—your cat is average (Yoiks!). Don't take offense—after all, it is the average that sets apart those who are "unusual," "different," etc. Many people prefer not to be unusual and they prefer their pets to be the same. We are sure that your kitty is quite special in many other ways. You need to be aware that your cat may be very psychic, very powerful, but is practicing its arts in many ways that are designed not to draw attention to itself. Cats know that when they are identified as powerful, they often suffer from those who are unenlightened, jealous, and even afraid. Well! Consider the ramifications.

If not, you have to accept the conclusion that your pussycat is, um, er, ah, "normal." Not all cats are involved in the paranormal, despite what you may have heard, or even believe to be true. Our extensive research in this area leads us to another conclusion. On the other hand, some have told us that (of course) all cats have psychic powers . . . don't they all read our minds and control our behavior in subtle ways? Scientifically, this seems no more than paranormal anthropomorphism, but then . . .

Moderately Low (77—157)

If your cat has psychic power, there is little evidence of it. This does not mean no power, just not very much. This animal can read your mind, of course, but not fully and not reliably. Some cats (and some owners) accept this limitation and seem content. Others rankle with the knowledge and they fidget and restlessly wander about, seemingly without purpose. We now know that these behaviors are readily understood as the agitated efforts to find new psychic meaning in their kitty lives. Some cats (usually black or mostly black) rebound with increased psychic power as they are able to contact their sources of potency. Sometimes their inability can be poignant and sadly frustrating, as when a cat will climb up on your lap and stare endlessly into your eyes . . . without any psychic exchange at all! They may want to blame us for our insensitivity, but psychic communication requires two to tango.

Low (0—76)

Can there be such a thing as a cat without psychic power? We have to say yes. These situations occur in highly unusual cases, usually when these felines are owned by engineers, accountants, or other such linear folks. Paranormal experts tell us that some of these kitties may possess powerful energy sources, but these messages simply bounce off the negative energy fields of the psychically challenged. Some use these as examples that there is no such thing as "pussycat psychic power" but our position is that not only should such assertions be discounted, these people should be actively avoided. Remember, a kitty which has no psychic power at all still makes a very fine pet!

ABOUT THE AUTHOR

Missy Dizick is a devoted cat watcher who is inspired by her "five rollicking pussycats," Loulou, Charlie, Bobby, Betty, and Weirdo. Her previous books include the controversial Cats Are Better Than Dogs, preceded by the disloyal Dogs Are Better Than Cats (coauthored with Mary Bly), which she is still trying to live down. Her prize-winning artwork appears on calendars and note cards and has been exhibited in galleries and museums in California and New York.

Ms. Dizick resides in Napa, California, where she has an absolutely smashing garden.